Where Lt. Colonel Weinstein has been featured:

Fitness Magazine
The History Channel
Fox Sports Net
Fox News Channel - Fox & Friends
The Washington Times
The Las Vegas Tribune
Eurosport TV
Gold Coast Magazine
Tropical Life Magazine Miami
The Sun-sentinel South Florida
The Miami Herald
USA Today
Oxygen Magazine
Univision
Telemundo
RAZOR Magazine
Boca Raton Magazine
Comcast Newsmakers
Army Times
Go Riverwalk Fort Lauderdale
WSFL The Morning Show
NBC Nonstop Miami
NBC6 South Florida Today
New Times Broward-Palm Beach
Navy League News - Fort Lauderdale Council
The Navy Leaguer
SoBeFit Magazine

The successful warrior is the average man with laser-like focus.

- Bruce Lee

QUOTES WISDOMS

And Some Dumb Things

Celebration of My Sixtieth

**Bob Weinstein
Lt. Colonel, U. S. Army, Retired
Boot Camp Fitness Instructor**

Health Colonel Publishing
www.BeachBootCamp.net

Colonel Bob's Blog:
ColonelBobsBeachBootCamp.blogspot.com/

Quotes, Wisdoms and Some Dumb Things: Celebration of My Sixtieth
By Lt. Colonel Bob Weinstein, U.S. Army, Retired.
Note: Bob is the nickname of Lt. Colonel Joseph R. Weinstein.
www.BeachBootCamp.net
Categories: self-help, love, advice, healing, inspirational, wisdom

Health Colonel Publishing
The Health Colonel Series™

Copyright © 2012 Joseph "Bob" Weinstein,
Lt. Colonel, U.S. Army, Retired.
All Rights Reserved.

ISBN-13: 978-1-935759-11-9
ISBN-10: 1-935759-11-6

Library of Congress Control Number: 2012933162

This book and parts thereof may not be reproduced in any form, stored in a retrieval system or transmitted in any form by any means (electronic, mechanical, photocopy, recording or otherwise) without prior written permission of the author, except as provided by United States of America copyright law.

Weinstein, Bob.
Weinstein, Joseph
Quotes, Wisdoms and Some Dumb Things: Celebration of My Sixtieth
/ by Joseph "Bob" Weinstein.– 1st ed.
ISBN-13: 978-1-935759-11-9 (trade pbk. : alk. Paper)
1. Self-Improvement–United States. I. Weinstein, Bob. Weinstein, Joseph.
II. Title. III. 60 Wisdoms
Printed in the United States

QUOTES WISDOMS

And Some Dumb Things

Celebration of My Sixtieth

**Bob Weinstein
Lt. Colonel, U. S. Army, Retired
Boot Camp Fitness Instructor**

**Health Colonel Publishing
www.BeachBootCamp.net**

**Colonel Bob's Blog:
ColonelBobsBeachBootCamp.blogspot.com/**

The successful person makes a habit of doing what the failing person doesn't like to do.
— Thomas Edison

ACKNOWLEDGEMENTS

Many thanks to all the
beach boot camp recruits on Fort Lauderdale Beach.
You remain a constant source of inspiration.
I thank you for your friendship and camaraderie.
You are my extended family.
May you prosper and enjoy a healthy and happy life.
A special thank you goes to my wife, Grit, who supports
me in all that I do. A special dedication to my son, David,
parents, brothers and sister.

Being fit and healthy has nothing to do with eating or exercise and has everything to do with how we think.

CONTENTS I

Introduction	13
Accountability	14
Aging or Getting Old	16
Alcohol	18
Art	20
Attitude	22
Beauty	24
Career	26
Character	28
Cigarettes	30
Civility	32
Compassion	34
Computers / Smartphones	36
Consumerism	38
Death	40
Disagreement	42
Email	44
Encouragement	46
Ethics	48
Exercise	50
Faith	52
Family	54
Food	56
Forgiveness	58
Frugality	60

CONTENTS II

Fun	62
Goals	64
God	66
Happiness	68
Honesty	70
Hope	72
Humility	74
Humor	76
Integrity	78
Kindness	80
Laughter	82
Leadership	84
Life	86
Love	88
Marriage	90
Money	92
Moral Courage	94
Music	96
Politics	98
Pornography	100
Purpose	102
Quiet Time	104
Race / Ethnicity	106
Relationships	108
Religion	110
Respect	112

CONTENTS III

Responsibility	114
Role Models	116
Servant	118
Service	120
Sex	122
Sorrow	124
Stimulation	126
Telephone	128
Thinking	130
Time	132
Titillation	134
Truth	136
Television	138
Work	140
About the Author	142
Other Books by the Author	144

INTRODUCTION

It seems like yesterday when I was growing up in Northern Virginia. That "yesterday" was in the 1950's, 60's and early part of the 1970's. With this book, I wanted to take a look back, take a look forward and to consider the now as well. It is a life-lessons-learned and assessment book, presented in such a way as to allow the reader to hopefully get some insight and ideas about how to live and make the right choices in life. My choices were not always right.

When I started working on 60 Wisdoms, I felt I had no real sense of my mortality until I was diagnosed with aggressive prostate cancer in November of 2011. It is now January 2012 and I am scheduled for surgery on January 17. It is interesting how such news can bring about a profound change in thinking, adding depth to thought about life and death. My first thought when I found out about the cancer is that I may not be on the earth as long as I thought. The good news is that the survival rate for prostate cancer is very high if caught in time which seems to be the case with me.

You may be asking yourself, "Why 60 Wisdoms." In the year 2011 I reached the ripe old age of sixty. Somehow I feel like anyone who reaches the age of sixty is old, except for me. Just kidding. I know people in their 20's or 40's or 50's who have become old by their outlook on life. In a sense, 60 Wisdoms, regardless of your age, should contribute to making you younger in how you think about yourself and others and life.

ACCOUNTABILITY

People think responsibility is hard to bear. It's not. I think that sometimes it is the absence of responsibility that is harder to bear. You have a great feeling of impotence.
— Henry Kissinger

ACCOUNTABILITY

Whether it's governments, families or individuals, accountability makes sure that we stay focused on what matters most, provides checks and balances. A sense of accountability towards my fellow man, woman, business partner, wife, son or daughter is essential. Life is not just about me. A me focused life is a lonely one and is not of benefit to others. There is an underlying reason why we need accountability in our lives. There is an inclination to follow self-gratifying desires and principles to the point of self-destruction. There is that desire to over-gratify with things, food, sex, drinking, drugs, music, free-time and even work. Self-gratification is self-centered and disregards those around us and those who are a part of our lives. If there is an area in your life lacking accountability that truly needs it, seek help and support to find the best way to incorporate accountability into that area.

AGING

I don't feel old. I don't feel anything till noon. That's when it's time for my nap.

— Bob Hope

AGING

It happens to be a fact of life that I am getting old. As a matter of fact, I'll bet it's happening to you too. I embrace it as a part of life. I take care of myself though I deviate from healthy eating habits from time to time. More important than getting old is how I am leading my life and what will my legacy be. How will I be remembered? If I were to die today, would I like what will be found in my obituary or do I need to make some adjustments so that my life focus is truly worthy? There are adjustments I need to make. I need to be focusing more on helping those in need. The attitude of my heart is most important since my motives do matter and that is something that only you and God can sort out. Society only sees what is going on on the outside, not the inside. There is more that I can do. There is more I can do in my everyday life as I interact with others while working, playing or driving to work.

ALCOHOL

I once shook hands with Pat Boone and my whole right side sobered up.

—Dean Martin

ALCOHOL

Moderate drinking is good, no alcohol is better. Through the years I have observed much social drinking become health issues, destroy families, friendships and careers. Any nutritional benefits to be gotten from alcohol can be found in the foods we eat. If, however, someone is dealing with a crisis that brings extreme burden on them emotionally, alcohol can certainly have a medicinal purpose. Beware of regular social drinking. That is where the trouble with alcohol begins and ends.

ART

Creativity is allowing yourself to make mistakes. Art is knowing which ones to keep.

—Scott Adams

ART

Art is food for the soul and a great way to practice and delve into ones creativity. The creation of art should be done with the forethought of benefiting oneself and others. There is art which is destructive and there is art which edifies the spirit and soul. There is art that will make us laugh, make us cry, make us angry, provoke thought, depict beauty, ugliness, simplicity, complexity, depth or superficiality. Art can touch on every human emotion and inspire us to great ideas or it can provoke us to have animosity towards people who are different from us or do not share our ideals.

ATTITUDE

Nothing can stop the man with the right mental attitude from achieving his goal; nothing on earth can help the man with the wrong mental attitude.

—Thomas Jefferson

ATTITUDE

Whether you are a man or a woman, old or young, black or white, democrat or republican, gay or straight, your attitude is the ultimate factor that determines your true outlook about yourself and how you treat others. Attitude is truly everything. Whatever views and opinions you may have, it is how you treat and talk about others who don't agree with you or your lifestyle that counts. Are you respectful? Are you courteous and kind? Do you care about others who don't embrace your views? I strive to treat all like my sons and daughters, brothers and sisters, fathers and mothers. Regardless of the views of my family members, I still care about them and avoid derogatory talk and disrespectful treatment.

BEAUTY

Beauty is a manifestation of secret natural laws, which otherwise would have been hidden from us forever.
—Johann Wolfgang von Goethe

BEAUTY

Is beauty just skin deep? True beauty is found inside and yet we may still admire external beauty. I once met a really ugly person who was one of the most beautiful people I've ever met. No, I,m not going to name her otherwise you might tell her I said she's ugly. She was cheerful, full of kindness and caring for everyone she met. Society's standards of who is more worthy or less did not apply. She equally honored and greeted everyone she came in contact with. My grandmother, Gammie, was similar except that she was physically a good looking woman. She always enjoyed cheering other people up. In the home for the elderly, where she was staying, both the staff and other residents encountered a regular dose of her humor, kindness and smile.

CAREER

A career is wonderful, but you can't curl up with it on a cold night.
—Marilyn Monroe

CAREER

What was your reason for choosing your career? Was it the money? Did your parents decide? Or is your career what you really wanted to do, your calling? There is nothing more powerful and invigorating than when we truly figure out what we really want to do in life. No money, no special privileges can ever replace the deep satisfaction of doing what you sense is your true destiny. If you're not there yet, find out what your true passion is and then do it. While pursuing your career, do not forget about those things and people money cannot buy.

CHARACTER

A man's character may be learned from the adjectives which he habitually uses in conversation.

—Mark Twain

CHARACTER

I'm sure you've heard the expression, "That's the way he is or that's the way she is." And I'm sure you may have said, "That's the way I am." The truth is all character traits are behaviors. All behaviors can be changed. The only one who can change your behavior is you. This is a wonderful piece of truth which means that there is hope for us who thought, "That's the way I am." Change that thought, "Here's who I want to be" and then start working on it. No matter how hard the task is, keep working on becoming the person you want to be.

CIGARETTES

It is common knowledge that smoking is considered one of the nation's leading causes of preventable death, but it's less widely known that cigarettes are also the leading cause of fatal fires.

—Ed Markey

CIGARETTES

Don't smoke cigarettes and, if you do, quit. With all the research about the dangers and special warning labels on cigarette packaging, we still have a significant number of people who smoke. Yes, it is an addiction and it's hard to quit. Get angry at the cigarettes, toss them out and save your life and the life of others. Secondary smoke also kills. The strong association of smoking and socializing and smoking and working makes the addiction very challenging to overcome. I don't believe in patches or anything that softens the quitting process. I believe we need to feel the pain of quitting in order to truly appreciate a life afterwards without cigarettes. Just quitting without all those fancy pain reducers will help strengthen your character. Other challenges in life will benefit from the struggle. My son smokes. I love him just the same.

CIVILITY

The civility which money will purchase, is rarely extended to those who have none.

—Charles Dickens

CIVILITY

I've heard this word bouncing around the media after the terrible shooting in Arizona when Congresswoman Gabrielle Giffords and others were shot. A call for civility in politics followed. Civility means debating and discourse without attacking the individual. We need civility in the media, at home, on the tennis courts, football fields, schools and wherever and however people interact with one another. True debate and the ability to evaluate the issues has been stifled by a lack of civility. Opposing opinions are considered targets to be attacked instead of listening and assessing them and not attacking the opposing opinionator. If an opinion deviates from the point of view of the other, the other will then say, "I hate ....." You can fill in the blank with the name of any group or individual that has an opposing view. This is wrong. A bad behavior example would be calling someone a racist because that someone wants stricter immigration policies.

COMPASSION

I can do no other than be reverent before everything that is called life. I can do no other than to have compassion for all that is called life. That is the beginning and the foundation of all ethics.

—Albert Schweitzer

COMPASSION

Have you ever felt like you needed some compassion? Everyone at some time in their lives will wish they would receive a little compassion, or a lot. Compassion never asks whether or not you earned or deserve compassion. Compassion is one of those great expressions of love. Compassion doesn't ask that you first be worthy. We all need to be on the lookout for opportunities to express compassion towards others, the deserved and the undeserved, the worthy and the unworthy, the wealthy and the poor, the sick and the healthy, the young and the old.

COMPUTERS / SMART PHONES

A computer once beat me at chess, but it was no match for me at kick boxing.

—Emo Philips

COMPUTERS / SMARTPHONES

We are becoming addicted to computers. We are checking our emails too frequently. We are checking various accounts too frequently. I am guilty of this behavior. Remember the days when there were no home computers and no smart phones? Some of you will remember and others will not. Somehow we survived. We are creating unnecessary stress in our lives by constantly having our computers / smart phones accessible and with us all the time. Observe those driving or walking. How many people do you see preoccupied with a cell phone or smart phone in the course of the day. Some will even walk through the check out line of the grocery store or order at Starbucks while making a phone call as if the call absolutely could not wait. Bring some sanity back into your life and manage the usage of computers and cell phones. If you don't, it will become a time waster and reduce your ability to concentrate on any one task or person.

CONSUMERISM

My first rule of consumerism is never to buy anything you can't make your children carry.

—Bill Bryson

CONSUMERISM

Consumerism has become the new religion of our modern society and it doesn't seem to make any difference whether we are financially well off or just getting by. Consumerism is a state of mind. Consumerism causes us to live beyond our means. Consumerism causes us to have less to give to help others who are needy. Sure, we are being influenced by a constant bombardment of advertising and being inflicted with the *I want what the Joneses have mentality.* Consumerism is the same kind of mechanism that causes us to overeat, be promiscuous with sex and seek a constant increase in gratification. Consumerism will rob you of the joys of life and may lead to too much debt and too many calories. Tone it down.

DEATH

Some people are so afraid to die that they never begin to live.
—Henry Van Dyke

DEATH

I am more concerned about having lived a fruitful and productive life focused on helping others than I am about dying. I do not know when or how I will die. I do know that I am going to die. Is there any purpose to giving thought to death and dying? Yes, I think there is. Contemplating my mortality helps me appreciate life much more. The thought of dying helps me to ask those deeper questions about why I am here and will there be a life after death? Will I be held accountable for my actions after death? Will there be judgment over the life that I led? I believe there will be. For this reason, I also believe it's paramount to seek out the creator of all that is and ever was until you find him. The attitude of your heart towards the creator and the created will play a decisive role.

Winston Churchill never lost his sense of humor, even on his deathbed, *"I am ready to meet my Maker. Whether my Maker is prepared for the great ordeal of meeting me is another matter."*

Comedian Spike Milligan's epitaph said: *"I told you I was ill."*

Crooner Frank Sinatra chose the title of one of his songs: *"The best is yet to come."*

DISAGREEMENT

Honest disagreement is often a good sign of progress.
—Mohandas Gandhi

DISAGREEMENT

We need to relearn the ability to disagree without being disrespectful. We need to relearn the ability to make the other person feel like he or she is still respected and valued even though we don't agree with that person on an issue or issues. There is so much name calling and attempts to belittle the person who has a differing view. The language is recognizable: idiot, hate, bitterness and more. This takes place in the media, politics and in the rest of society. This is what causes polemics and a polarization of views. Whatever happened to the basic ground rules of a debate without attacking the person, without belittling the person or their views? Whatever happened to shaking hands before and after? Whatever happened to statements such as, "I don't agree with you, but I can understand that there are worthy aspects that need to be honored and protected." Or how about this one? "That is my view on this issue but I may be wrong."

EMAIL

Men won't read any email from a woman that's over 200 words long.
—Doug Coupland

EMAIL

Let's spend more face time instead of Facebook or email time. Don't get me wrong. I use all the various modern forms of communication from online social networking to emails to text messaging and blogging. None of this replaces the timeless form of spending time with someone, listening and sharing with them.

ENCOURAGEMENT

Nine tenths of education is encouragement.
—Anatole France

ENCOURAGEMENT

Encouragement keeps us going when we don't feel like it and empowers us to do great things, one small step at a time. Be a self-encourager and always encourage others to do the right thing.

ETHICS

Ethics is knowing the difference between what you have a right to do and what is right to do.
—Potter Stewart

ETHICS

It is interesting that ethics is mostly discussed when it's about the other guy when in fact I am the least common denominator of ethics. Just the other day I was asked by someone to engage in a business transaction that would have violated an agreement I have with a business. The person on the phone said, "They won't find out." I agreed and said that it would not be right to violate the agreement. Since it was about financial gain for me, there was some temptation to say yes. But I sure feel better for honoring my agreement and being honest in my dealings with all parties. Our society has a certain cultural climate that takes ethics lightly if no one is watching. Being ethical is something that is done whether someone is watching or not. Something negative happens to me in my soul when I am unethical. Something positive happens to my soul when I am ethical in my dealings both private and in business.

EXERCISE

Yes, exercise is the catalyst. That's what makes everything happen: your digestion, your elimination, your sex life, your skin, hair, everything about you depends on circulation.

—Jack LaLanne

EXERCISE

We've heard it again and again. Eat right and exercise. Movement of the body is the key. You must develop a philosophy of movement. This will prevent too much TV or computer time or too much time spent with computer games or smart phones. Plan for five to seven hours of exercise and movement based activities per week. It will prevent diseases, such as heart attack, cancer, stroke or diabetes. Our bodies need oxygen. Better cardio conditioning through movement improves the body's ability to process oxygen. If we lead a sedentary lifestyle we shorten our lives and open the door to an array of diseases and illnesses that diminish the quality of our lives.

FAITH

Faith has to do with things that are not seen and hope with things that are not at hand.

—Thomas Aquinas

FAITH

Faith is believing even though we don't have all of the facts or they are simply out of reach. Do we really know that we will wake up the next morning when going to sleep? Do we know for certain that our loved ones will return from work or shopping? Do we know our car will start the next time we get in. Do I know that I will be alive tomorrow, next week or a year from now? I don't know any of this. I have faith. My faith in God as the Creator is the same. I see evidence of his work everywhere. I see it in science, math, music and the arts. I sense a higher moral authority that has planted his values in my heart. Although I do not see God, I seek and therefore sense his presence. The very plausibility of his existence is based on the very existence and structure of all that we know about our universe and our planet with its inhabitants. In your faith journey, you may still be seeking out the truth. Please remain a seeker and open your heart so that the Creator can have an opportunity to make his presence known to you. Ask Him for clarity and faith.

FAMILY

A man should never neglect his family for business.

—*Walt Disney*

FAMILY

Strong family ties based on sound moral values is the very foundation for a healthy society, healthy adults and healthy children. I did volunteer work for the Covenant House which helps homeless and runaway youth. I had the wonderful opportunity to speak with many of them who were ages 14 to 17. There was a broken family behind each of the stories. These kids were hungry for someone who cared. Many of them had lost faith in people because of their experiences. I remember speaking with one of the kids about how he came to be at the Covenant House. He responded, "My mother didn't want me anymore." I was devastated by his response while trying to maintain my composure. There is a lot of hurt in the world due to broken families resulting from verbal and physical abuse. I believe in many instances that the verbal abuse can be much more destructive and long-lasting. Work on mending family ties wherever and however possible. Start today with a phone call or a letter. Never underestimate the power of reaching out to heal a relationship without creating any demands on the family member. You are already letting them know you care about them simply by reaching out.

FOOD

A house is not a home unless it contains food and fire for the mind as well as the body.
—Benjamin Franklin

FOOD

If you eat too much sugar and fat in your diet and do it regularly, you are addicted. You will want more sugar and fat. If you are addicted and you happen to be especially stressed you will - like most of us in this situation - eat more sugar and fat which means more of the foods that are high in sugar and fat. Don't get me wrong. These types of foods taste really good. But the unfortunate truth is that they will kill you. It is a slow death which means your bad health and the ensuing diseases such as heart attack, stroke, diabetes and cancer are already festering inside of you. No, you won't feel ill effects for a while. You will just nurture the necessary bad health that will lead to illness and a shortened life span. Go to the refrigerator right now or look carefully at what you order when you go to a restaurant. What do you see? What are you eating on a regular basis? If need be, scare yourself into making a change. I can assure you that fruits and vegetables are the way to go and they also taste great once you wean yourself off the sugar and fat addictions. Stay away from meat and reduce the dairy as much as you can. You'll get plenty of protein from other plant sources (nuts, brown rice, grains and others). Fish is a good choice at least twice a week as long as you avoid the predatory fish and stay away from the farm raised fish as well. Get six to eight glasses of water a day, avoid alcohol and minimize or eliminate caffeine intake. Eat at least three regular meals with about two healthy snacks a day. Depending on your activity level, you may have to increase or decrease your caloric intake. Your waistline will be a dead giveaway if you are taking in too many calories.

FORGIVENESS

Forgiveness is the economy of the heart... forgiveness saves the expense of anger, the cost of hatred, the waste of spirits.
—Hannah More

FORGIVENESS

We all have a need to be forgiven and we have a need to forgive. If you do not forgive, you will suffer the consequences in your mind, body and soul. It will leave you with festering negative thoughts that will harm your health, rob you of energy, make you unhappy and weaken your performance and productivity.

FRUGALITY

I hold it the duty of the executive to insist upon frugality in the expenditure, and a sparing economy is itself a great national source.
—Andrew Johnson

FRUGALITY

This is a word we rarely hear in our society. We usually think of frugality as living the simple life, sticking with the less expensive choices. Living under what we earn regardless of what we earn. There is a mentality in our culture that makes us immediately go out and get the bigger, better car or house or whatever it may be that we like to spend money on as soon as our earnings increase. This would not be an issue if frugality is applied. We would not be seriously in debt, we would not have problems with our bills and we would have the necessary reserves of funds in times of emergencies. We would also have more to help those who are less fortunate than us.

FUN

People rarely succeed unless they have fun in what they are doing.
—*Dale Carnegie*

FUN

All we want to do is have a little fun in life. What is fun? Fun is a state of mind. You can have fun and work and be fun to work with. You can have fun at home and be fun to live with. You can have fun with your friends and be fun to have fun with. You can have fun with your spouse and children and they will have fun with you. Fun is a state of mind that makes living much more enjoyable. True fun does not depend upon external situations or circumstances.

GOALS

Crystallize your goals. Make a plan for achieving them and set yourself a deadline. Then, with supreme confidence, determination and disregard for obstacles and other people's criticisms, carry out your plan.

—Paul J. Meyer

GOALS

Big goals drive the little goals just as subtasks are driven by tasks. I always like asking the question. What is more important, long-term or short-term goals? Some will say short-term goals, others will say long-term. They both are not right. The entire marketing industry feeds off our desire for quick gratification. That is what may make us think that short-term goals are more important. Long-term goals that we have truly embraced are the ones that really keep us on track or get us back on track. By the way, no long-term goal is a goal, too and will lead to wherever it may take you like a ship without sails. Of course we will use short-term goals in the process and that is good as long as we are doing it because of the embraced long-term goal. For example, you want to lose 20 pounds over the next three months. That is a short-term goal. A worthy long-term goal would be to maintain a healthy lifestyle which includes managing your weight. Understanding and embracing all the health benefits of this long-term goal is a strong driving force to keep you on track even though there may be setbacks along the way.

GOD

We need to find God, and he cannot be found in noise and restlessness. God is the friend of silence. See how nature - trees, flowers, grass- grows in silence; see the stars, the moon and the sun, how they move in silence... We need silence to be able to touch souls.

—Mother Teresa

GOD

It seems as though God has become more of a political point of debate of whether or not it's correct to talk about Him or mention Him in public. I don't know whether that is the proper respect for the Creator of the universe and all that is and ever was. Natural discussion about God and the meaning of life should be as normal as taking a shower and brushing your teeth except that it is more important. Dealing with the question of God deals with the fundamental questions of who we are, what our purpose is, where we came from and where we are going. Those are underlying questions that are coupled with natural laws. From those laws emanate our values. They can be found in our heart if we are willing to dig deep, if we are willing to search, if we are willing to listen and ask the important life questions instead of shunning them. We always talk about respecting one another. Doesn't God deserve this respect as well?

HAPPINESS

We hold these truths to be self-evident: that all men are created equal; that they are endowed by their Creator with certain unalienable rights; that among these are life, liberty, and the pursuit of happiness.
—Thomas Jefferson

HAPPINESS

Does anyone really know what happiness is? What determines your happiness? Is it a person or career or a certain hobby? What if you no longer have that certain person, career or hobby in your life? Does that mean you can no longer be happy? Happiness should be much more than a person or persons in your life, a career or a hobby. True happiness is independent of all external circumstances, people or things or careers. Happiness is a state of mind, a decision. True happiness is focusing on helping others. That focus is internal and is expressed externally. You decide to focus on helping others and you then act on that decision every day of your life. Your first step in helping others is to be a cheerful, friendly and courteous person. Your next step is to identify needs that are within your means to fulfill and then go out and help. By the way, that approach makes God happy, too.

HONESTY

All men profess honesty as long as they can. To believe all men are honest would be folly. To believe none so is something worse.
—John Quincy Adams

HONESTY

All areas of our lives will benefit from honesty and of course honesty starts with me. If I were to tell you that I never told a lie, that would be the biggest lie I ever told. If there is anyone out there who has never told a lie, I would like to meet them and I'm skeptical about whether that human being exists. Honesty builds trust, dishonesty breaks it down. The health of any relationship is based on honesty. There is nothing more valuable than an employee who is honest with the boss. There is nothing more valuable than a boss who is honest with employees. Good customer service depends upon honesty towards the customers and clients.

HOPE

We must accept finite disappointment, but never lose infinite hope.

—Martin Luther King, Jr.

HOPE

Hope is that little voice inside that keeps saying, "You're going to make it. You're going to get through." There are times when things get really tough. Financial debt, divorce, infidelity, homelessness, natural disasters, major exam, unemployment, loneliness, illness, death in the family, serious injury, drug addiction, alcohol abuse and the list goes on. We all perceive difficulties and challenges differently. That is important to understand. We seem to think of hope as being intangible when in fact the result of hope - or the lack thereof - has a tremendous concrete influence on what we will do in the given challenging situation. A feeling of hopelessness will incapacitate us to undertake nothing. Hope, on the other hand, will empower us to find ways to continue on and ideas to perhaps overcome the challenge more quickly. Do you think that the lack of hope on the part of a commander of military forces will potentially cause the loss of his soldiers or the loss of the battle? I think so.

HUMILITY

Do you wish to rise? Begin by descending. You plan a tower that will pierce the clouds? Lay first the foundation of humility.

—Saint Augustine

HUMILITY

Humility is a great strength and not a weakness. Pride does not have our fellow man and woman in mind and is the opposite of humility. A humble person is less focused on him- or herself and more focused on others. A humble person takes nothing personal and gives everyone the benefit of the doubt. A humble person does not boast and brag and put other people down or put them on the spot.

HUMOR

A person without a sense of humor is like a wagon without springs. It's jolted by every pebble on the road.
—Henry Ward Beecher

HUMOR

I have a "pebble" in my road right now and it is called prostate cancer. As I mentioned in the introduction part of this book, I will have surgery on January 17, 2012. Other pebbles in the road could be unfriendly or even insulting behavior of someone you meet or someone you know. It could be that job you just lost or an investment that just went south on you. Humor in no way negates or lessons the seriousness of bad things that happen to us. Humor does, however, lighten the load. I have heard stories of soldiers who fought in battles during World War II with death, blood, gun fire, artillery and mortar shells exploding around them who were able to maintain their composure with humor in not-so-humorous situations. Humor is a stress and anxiety reliever. There are situations where humor may not be appropriate such as during a time of grief when a loved one passes away or is seriously ill. Or someone we know may need some compassion and caring at a certain time and other times a cheering up. The exact health benefits of the use of humor are not all substantiated. However, one thing is for sure, humor makes us feel good. That is the reason why humor sells when it comes to the entertainment industry. I think we can think of several comedians who would agree with this statement.

INTEGRITY

A life lived with integrity – even if it lacks the trappings of fame and fortune is a shining star in whose light others may follow in the years to come.

—Denis Waitley

INTEGRITY

There is nothing more refreshing than to get an honest, straightforward answer even if it is not what I want to hear. There is nothing better than being honest and up front in both our business and private dealings. We all hear about the reputations of people. Let's acquire the reputation of being a person of integrity. Both our words and our deeds can be trusted. We all should strive to be a person of integrity.

KINDNESS

A tree is known by its fruit; a man by his deeds. A good deed is never lost; he who sows courtesy reaps friendship, and he who plants kindness gathers love.
—Saint Basil

KINDNESS

Kindness is priceless. Some of us figure things out faster. Others need to make more mistakes along the way. Regardless of your life journey, words and deeds of kindness will brighten up the life of others and your life as well. Kindness has a wonderful healing impact not only on the one expressing kindness but on the recipient. Kindness heals mentally and physically. Kindness will boost the immune system and relaxes the blood pressure.

LAUGHTER

Joy in one's heart and some laughter on one's lips is a sign that the person down deep has a pretty good grasp of life.

—Hugh Sidey

LAUGHTER

Laughter is another great gift of God that helps us not to take life too seriously, but serious enough to live by the Golden Rule and focus on doing what is right. I am going to distinguish between different types of laughter based on my life experiences and observations. The type of laughter I am talking about is the the wholesome and positive laughter that means no harm to oneself or anyone else. The laughter I am not talking about is the one that is hollow and, at times, sinister which is neither healthy for the laugher nor the "laughee," that is the one who hears the negative laughter; this type of laughter is not really genuine and is destructive. Genuine laughter is uplifting for the one laughing and those who are around him or her. Genuine laughter reduces stress hormones and is a great physical and mental release. Laughter can distract from such emotions as anger, fear, overwhelming guilt or other negative emotions. If you are in any of these emotional situations, seek out opportunities for some wholesome laughter. You may find that you are then better focused and more able to deal with the situation at hand as a positive challenge rather than as a threat.

LEADERSHIP

A good objective of leadership is to help those who are doing poorly to do well and to help those who are doing well to do even better.
—Jim Rohn

LEADERSHIP

We are all leaders. As soon as we interact with others we become role models for how to live and how to treat others. Once we truly understand this, we begin to make positive adjustments on how we think and how we influence others. We have heard the expression, "Follow the leader." Who is the leader? Where is he or she taking me? Is this good for me? Why should I follow? What kind of person will I become? What kind of role model are you? What do others see when they observe you in their daily lives? Are your expressed and practiced values something you would have others do?

LIFE

Every man dies. Not every man really lives.

—William Wallace

LIFE

What is life all about? Where will it take me? What can I do to make life better for me and for others? What is the purpose of life? Am I a positive contributor? There is something instilled within us that will allow us to answer such questions or at least take us in the right direction. There is direction and there is purpose. Listen to your heart, be honest with yourself and be a seeker of truth and you will find it.

LOVE

At the touch of love everyone becomes a poet.

—*Plato*

LOVE

Some of us guys still cringe a little when this word is used a little too much. Love is foundational. Love is not just a feeling. Love is a way to act and think about and towards others. Every act of kindness and caring is an act of love. Courtesies, such as holding the door for someone or being kind to those who may be in the process of insulting you or treating you poorly, are acts of love. The ancient prophet Moses understood the foundational meaning of love, not just towards each other but also towards the creator of all that is. Jesus understood the true meaning of love. Gandhi understood the true meaning of love. Martin Luther King understood the true meaning of love. Next time you hear someone say they don't "feel" the love, you will now understand that love is more than a feeling.

MARRIAGE

What counts in making a happy marriage is not so much how compatible you are, but how you deal with incompatibility.
—Leo Tolstoy

MARRIAGE

Marriage is a special lifetime commitment of love and caring. I have made my mistakes along the way throughout life with this one. I have remarried and, I believe, for all the right reasons. Marriage is sacred and not a throw-away product. People are sacred and not throw-away products.

MONEY

Money isn't the most important thing in life, but it's reasonably close to oxygen on the "gotta have it" scale.
—Zig Ziglar

MONEY

Money is the root of all evil. Right? Wrong! The love and over-attachment to money is evil and destructive, not money. Our relationship to money can be healthy or unhealthy. It is unhealthy when we do not respect money. If we don't respect money, it will leave us. How do we disrespect money? We disrespect it by treating it like a throw-away product, as if it simply grows on trees and no concern for tomorrow is necessary. Many complain of not having any savings. The predominant reason they don't have savings is they are not saving. Whatever we earn there is always the ability to save a percentage of that income. We live in a culture of consumerism. It has become a form of religion. Whether it's food, clothing, books, jewelry, cars, boats, stereos, TVs or something else, consumerism is the drug of our present society. Take heart. You can turn this one around and fight the consumerism mentality and rekindle your respect for money. And make sure you put aside 10 percent of your money for those less fortunate.

MORAL COURAGE

What everyone else is doing is quite irrelevant when it comes to doing what is right.

—Russell Gough

MORAL COURAGE

As a senior instructor with the U. S. Army Command & General Staff College, I attended a command briefing at the U. S. Southern Command (SOUTHCOM) in South Florida. General Wilhelm, the SOUTHCOM Commander at the time, conducted the briefing. He talked about physical and moral courage using a story to illustrate the two. As the illustration goes, give me 10 men and women in uniform and order them to attack an enemy machine gun position. Of those 10 soldiers, 8 of them carry out those orders without hesitation even though they would probably be killed or wounded. Take those same 10 men and women and put them in a conference room listening to the General present an erroneous idea and - in all probability - only 2 out of 10 soldiers would question that idea. General Wilhelm as SOUTHCOM Commander welcomed discussion and debate which ensured that the best decisions and ideas were utilized. We need to be willing to have the moral courage to speak up while remaining respectful whether you are talking to a loved one, friend, boss, commanding officer or stranger. Moral courage has something to do with saying what we perceive to be right to stop the erroneous. Do not be concerned about whether your idea will be accepted or rejected. Moral courage is not concerned about that.

MUSIC

I was born with music inside me. Music was one of my parts. Like my ribs, my kidneys, my liver, my heart. Like my blood. It was a force already within me when I arrived on the scene. It was a necessity for me-like food or water.

—Ray Charles

MUSIC

Every man, woman and child should learn to sing or play an instrument. Music is an enrichment for the mind, body and soul. At the same time, be careful about the content of the music you play and listen to on a regular basis. I'm not going to pass judgment on any type of music. The message of a song and its melody can differ. Not all lyrics are beneficial for me or others. I listen to classical music, rock, blues, jazz and others. I always ask myself what the music will do to my outlook on life? Is it portraying a lifestyle that benefits me and others if I were to adapt the lifestyle portrayed?

POLITICS

Free speech is not to be regulated like diseased cattle and impure butter. The audience that hissed yesterday may applaud today, even for the same performance.

—William O. Douglas

POLITICS

It is interesting to observe that politics is viewed with a hefty dose of cynicism regardless of political affiliation. Political parties seem to be quick to criticize and slow to acknowledge common ground or mistakes. My view on politics? Politics and politicians are necessary in our democratic society. I have met both liberals and conservatives I respect and admire. What do I admire about them? Those I admire the most are the ones who predominantly focus on the issues, are respectful when talking with or about the other party or those with opposing views. Is the primary focus on caring about others or getting re-elected? I have nothing against a politician being interested in re-election. Every decision and policy has long- and short-term consequences. Are they taken adequately into consideration or is there too much focus on short-term benefit? I observe a tendency to appease in the short-term. It reminds me of all those weight loss programs offering up a quick solution for weight loss while disregarding the all important lifestyle aspect, long-term solution. Unfortunately, the media has fueled and incited the negative behavior of attacking the person more than focusing on the issues. I do need to mention that some in the media do indeed focus on the issues and spend more time exploring concrete arguments for policy issues portrayed.

PORNOGRAPHY

Most x-rated films are advertised as "adult entertainment," for "mature adults," when in reality they are juvenile entertainment for immature and insecure people.

—Zig Ziglar

PORNOGRAPHY

Talking about pornography is always going to hit a hot button. Pornography feeds on our desire for pleasure. I too have looked at pornography and have had issues with too frequent looking. Statistics have shown that a predominant percentage of men who attend church have accessed pornography on the internet, and not by accident. Pornography is a relationship killer. It robs a part of us that should be more focused on caring about and helping others and that does not mean only people who agree with our view about life. The pleasure seeking part of us gets out of control which makes for a more self-centered person. An over-emphasis of pleasure seeking and pleasure experiencing is self-centered behavior and can lead to psychological addiction which requires a frequent and high level of accountability to overcome. If we think carefully we can see the same parallels in other areas of our lives when it comes to pleasure, such as overeating, sweets, alcohol, drugs, gambling, physical appearance and any other area with an unhealthy constant over-emphasis of pleasure.

PURPOSE

Our prime purpose in this life is to help others. And if you can't help them, at least don't hurt them.
—Dalai Lama

PURPOSE

Do you know where you're headed in life? Are you clear about the person you would like to become? Or do you just let life happen to you? Are you looking for a job or are you looking for a career in an area that matches your natural gifts that are inherent within you? Do you know where your true passions lie? Is your job, service or product of benefit to other people and society as a whole? Or does it break down societal structures of family, friends and country? Do you know which character and life values are inalienable and should be included in your overall purpose? Do you know why you exist and for what purpose? There are two basic purposes. One is the general purpose that applies to all of us and then there is the more special purpose that applies to the individual. We need to seek and discover both. The special purpose brings together your individual talents and gifts so that your individual purpose in society is fulfilled.

QUIET TIME

We need quiet time to examine our lives openly and honestly. . . spending quiet time alone gives your mind an opportunity to renew itself and create order.

—Susan L. Taylor

QUIET TIME

Does anyone remember the days when we did not walk around with a cell phone because they didn't exist? I go back to the time when the only online social networking that existed was the telephone party line. Party lines existed during the days when there were not enough land line telephone numbers available so you shared one with several other households. Each household on the party line had a distinctive ring although all households on the party line could pick up the phone and take the call on purpose or by accident.

Find time to get away from all those gadgets and distractions to get a healthy dose of quiet time on a regular basis.

RACE AND ETHNICITY

Gentleness, self-sacrifice and generosity are the exclusive possession of no one race or religion.
—Mohandas Gandhi

RACE AND ETHNICITY

I remember back in the days of high school which, by the way, was a very long time ago. Anyone who was too big, too small, too skinny, too fat, too beautiful, too ugly, too intelligent, too dumb, too shy or too outgoing or looked different due to color was not treated as if he or she belonged. Don't get me wrong. This was not always the case. There were also many students who treated all others with respect and dignity. We humans do have a tendency to view anything that makes a person different with some suspicion. What's the real issue with race discrimination? The real issue is the true value of every human being sometimes gets lost in the differences. For those that believe in a clear chain of command which starts with respect and reverence for the Creator and a clear understanding of the high value he places on all of us regardless our color or any other differences, any lessoning of the value of any human being is a violation of the highest natural law. That highest natural law is to love and respect the Creator with all your heart and soul and to equally love and respect all others. Sometimes we all have a tendency to forget that you and I are also "all others." That means the natural law says you are to love and respect yourself the same way. Why? If you don't, it will influence how you treat others.

RELATIONSHIPS

Oh, the comfort – the inexpressible comfort of feeling safe with a person – having neither to weigh thoughts nor measure words, but pouring them all right out, just as they are, chaff and grain together; certain that a faithful hand will take and sift them, keep what is worth keeping, and then with the breath of kindness blow the rest away.
—*Dinah Craik, A Life for a Life, 1859*

RELATIONSHIPS

Many decades ago there was a study conducted on infants in an orphanage. The purpose of the study was to find out if the expression of love and affection or the lack thereof played a role in the lives of children. These children received food, clothing and any other material needs. They did not receive any expressed love or affection. After a while these children became withdrawn, came down with illnesses and died at a much higher frequency than the group of children that received expressed love and affection. What does this tell us? This tells us that we are social beings. The quality of our relationships at work, at home, growing up and as adults, will influence our well-being and influence how we interact with others. Seek out sound relationships and you will be much happier and probably have better health. Conversely, your ability to nurture quality relationships will, in many cases, result in you finding others who will do the same. You will be surprised to find out that, in many cases, it will be reciprocated.

RELIGION

A religious man is a person who holds God and man in one thought at one time, at all times, who suffers harm done to others, whose greatest passion is compassion, whose greatest strength is love and defiance of despair.

—Abraham Joshua Heschel

When I was in elementary school I wrote an essay about God. I described how man saw lightning strike from the heavens and, out of this experience, man created God. I further assessed the world situation with people as I knew of it at that time and came to the conclusion in my essay, that, if there is a God, he needs to wipe out all mankind and start over. My elementary school teacher was very upset with my essay. She was of the Christian faith and took her faith seriously. Instead of using my essay to further discuss my view, she simply became upset and did not really know how to respond. How I would have welcomed that discussion instead of her getting upset.

RELIGION

A healthy discussion without being judgmental is always helpful along our journey through life. I respect everyone 's view on life and am interested in finding out how they arrived at their view. In my lifetime, I have been an agnostic, atheist, have explored some ancient Asiatic religions and in the past many years have become someone who believes the story about God becoming man and sacrificing himself in place of us for our violations of his moral laws, also called sins. Since then, I have not always been on track and have needed forgiveness for my own wrongdoings towards others. I think I was on track as a kid in elementary school when I recognized that it is tough for us humans to do the right thing and that their is a lot of self-interest, hate and selfishness in this world.

There is a rebellious heart that needs to be changed through forgiveness and a sense of humility towards others. I believe that the laws of God are written on our hearts and can be summed up in this law which Moses and Jesus both stated as being the ultimate law to govern our lives. That law states, in my words, that we are to love God with all our hearts and souls and we are to love all others <u>just the same</u>. There's no picking and choosing who to love with God's love and who not to love. We fulfill all of God's laws if we fulfill this one. We violate all of God's laws if we violate this one.

RESPECT

Without feelings of respect, what is there to distinguish men from beasts?

—Confucius

RESPECT

I was visiting my great aunt Erlie at the assisted living home where she was staying. She was well over 80 years old. We were sitting outside talking when one of the residents stopped by on his scooter chair. His name was Bob and owned his own plumbing business before he could no longer walk without assistance. Now Bob was also in his eighties. Aunt Erlie introduced Bob the plumber. Looking at his situation I mustered the courage to ask him how he likes living in the home. Surprisingly, Bob the plumber replied, "I love it here." So I had to ask, "What do you like about it?" He replied, "I have all these people I can help. I was pretty good at working with my hands so I went out and bought an old used sewing machine for $20. I rode around on my scooter chair from room to room bringing coffee and spending time talking. Most of all I offered to make customized pouches and hand bags that would attach to the walkers, wheelchairs and canes. I supplied the material and personally made the items using my used sewing machine." Bob the plumber could have focused on the negative aspects of his situation but chose instead to focus on helping others. He did not see his problems. He only saw all these people who could use his help. By going room to room to see what he could do to help with his old used sewing machine really sent a more important message to those living in the home. That message was, "I care about you. You are worthy of respect and care."

RESPONSIBILITY

You must take personal responsibility. You cannot change the circumstances, the seasons, or the wind, but you can change yourself. That is something you have charge of.
—Jim Rohn

RESPONSIBILITY

A few years ago, I was training 12 to 21 year olds on the beach with a military-style fitness boot camp in Fort Lauderdale, Florida. These juveniles were staying at one of the homes of the Covenant House which offers homeless and runaway kids a place to stay, meals and a chance to get their lives together with schooling and other training. I happened to catch one of the kids mentioning that he is on suspension for something he did at the lunch table with other kids. One of the kids said something really insulting so he threw his sandwich in the face of the other kid. That's why he's on suspension. I asked him if there is anything he learned from the experience. He said he learned to better control his emotions. This particular kid was really impulsive but made no excuses for what he had done. He took responsibility for his action. He could have focused on the really insulting name calling which would have robbed him of the chance to take responsibility for his action. He also understood that managing his emotions is still an area of his life that is a work in progress. He said to me, "Colonel Bob, I'm much better than I was in the past." This 17 year old not only took responsibility but engaged in self assessment of his behavior. He was farther ahead than many adults.

ROLE MODELS

Role models and social influences have an effect on our self image; choosing good role models is crucial to our success.

—Brian Tracy

There is a lot of talk about role models. Most of the talk relates to our youth, some to adults. One thing is for sure. We all model behavior of others in some way. We all need good role models. Some will admit this and others are in denial. What kind of role models do we need? In our society this may very well be a multicultural and multi-political question. Underneath our political, religious and cultural views, there is - in my view - a list of values that should not be influenced by our view-of-life leanings. In secular terms, it is called the Golden rule. Most cultures around the world recognize the Golden Rule as foundational for how people interact with each other in any society. The Golden Rule states that you should do (and say) unto others as you would have them do (and say) unto you. That immediately eliminates any hate, animosity or bitterness in word and deed. This applies to oneself as well so there is no way to pervert the Golden Rule with such a philosophy as, "I don't treat myself well and therefore I will do the same to others." The Golden Rule exists with the underlying premise that there is indeed right and wrong. What are some other descriptive words for behaviors that are worthy of role modeling?

ROLE MODELS

Here are a few: honesty, respect, patience, humility, politeness, integrity, responsibility, caring, fairness, trustworthiness, forgiveness, graciousness and many others. It seems we are experiencing a drought when it comes to behavior or emulating the Golden Rule in our society and others as well. In this age of Twitter, Facebook, emails, blogs, the World Wide Web, YouTube, MySpace, and iPhones, there are powerful means to quickly disseminate behavior that is worthy of role modeling and other behavior that is not. Our other mass means of media such as television, newspapers and magazines are the areas that bombard us - for better or worse - with behaviors that many times blatantly violate the Golden Rule which means there is more focus on name calling and attempting to discredit someone somewhere rather than focusing on the issues. That is not only disrespectful but is also an indication of lack of integrity. Freedom of expression and press should not be a license to operate outside of the realm of the Golden Rule. I spent twenty years in Berlin, Germany from 1975 to 1995. The East German media was an extended arm of the regime under communist rule and was not interested in the issues but following an agenda. The media in our democratic societies should not emulate this behavior since it degrades what we strive to stand for. Any dictatorship or democracy or any other system of government whether coming from the right or the left or any other direction can run the risk of violating the Golden Rule by treating it like it doesn't exist.

SERVANT

He sat down, called the twelve disciples over to him, and said, "Whoever wants to be first must take last place and be the servant of everyone else."
—Jesus Christ, Mark 9:35
New Living Translation

SERVANT

There are a couple of things that come to mind when we use the word servant. We may think of slavery or we may think of servitude as in mandatory labor of any form. The servant I am talking about is the one based on an attitude towards all people we come in contact with. I cannot think of any better example than the one from Jesus of Nazareth. His apostles were arguing about which of them would be the greatest in the Kingdom of God. Jesus said anyone who strives to be the greatest must become a servant to all. Now that's behavior to emulate.

SERVICE

Service which is rendered without joy helps neither the servant nor the served. But all other pleasures and possessions pale into nothingness before service which is rendered in a spirit of joy.

—Mohandas Gandhi

SERVICE

How do you want to be remembered when all is said and done on this Earth? Hard worker? Fun to be with? Family man or woman? Party goer? Drinker? Workaholic? Business man or woman? Womanizer? How about someone who made it his or her mission to serve others? Serving and service is a state of mind followed by specific action. A service minded person seeks and finds opportunities to help others in a beneficial way whether at work or at home. A service minded person who works in the corporate world as a white collar worker finds ways to enhance the life of other workers. A service minded blue collar worker does just the same. I'm sure you can think of people at work who gave that extra something to serve others. Think of a person now who left a special impression as being someone who was particularly interested in sincerely serving others. What did this person of service do that made you come to this conclusion? Was it just their deeds or was there a certain attitude of the heart? Become service minded at work and at home. Find ways to make the life of others better. Find time even if it is just one hour per week to volunteer to help those who have very special needs: the homeless, the elderly, troubled youth, orphans or anyone who is destitute. Remember, no one is asking you to do more than you are capable of doing. Everyone can free up an hour to volunteer to serve others. Get out and serve.

SEX

> *I blame my mother for my poor sex life. All she told me was 'the man goes on top and the woman underneath.' For three years my husband and I slept in bunk beds.*
>
> —Joan Rivers

I wasn't sure I really wanted to include sex as one of the areas. The truth is we are bombarded with sex related marketing and news and social networking, talk at work, talk at home. Then there is YouTube and television, iPhones and eMails, twittering. I think "bombarded" is the best way to describe how we are confronted with sex. There is a certain viewpoint that has been propagated and that is, if it feels good, do it. We are sexual beings so we also need to know how to think about and treat sex. We also need to know how to appropriately talk to our children about sex and not just leave it to the street talk and other means. It's interesting how quickly sex becomes the deciding factor for getting involved in a relationship. The truth is if sex becomes a basis before there is long-term commitment, it will impede the ability to determine those aspects of the relationship that are more important than sex. I too have made the statement that great sex is an important deciding factor for a good relationship at certain times in my life and have paid the price for such thought. Does that mean that the relationship is no longer good if the sex is no longer good? Does this mean that great sex equates to a great relationship? Of course not!

SEX

I do believe that there is a basic predetermined order of things in that sex is reserved for humans between a man and a woman. I don't want to disregard the fact that we have those who are born with inclinations towards the same-sex. Then again there are those who have empirically adopted sexual behavior towards the same sex or for that matter, both sexes or just plain sex in any form. I honestly cannot decide which is the case. Even though I don't consider same-sex relationships the basic order of things, I do fully recognize the sincere affection and love that transcends any thought of sex between people. I hope all my friends are big enough to accept me with how I think about this topic whether they agree with me or not. How we treat each other has nothing whatsoever to do with sex and everything to do with those higher values which include how we are to treat every human being on this earth with respect and kindness. At the same time, for those who do not agree with this basic order of things as I do, I hope you will also recognize the right of parents to up-bring their children with such values. If there would be such reciprocal respect, we would not have the level of intolerance propagated in society, in the media and in politics. Intolerance as well as respect or the lack thereof goes in both directions. Tolerating does not mean agreeing with the position of the other. Respect does mean appreciating the value of those who do not agree with you and treating them accordingly. Our society has lost its ability for healthy debate that does not attack the person but focuses on the issue at hand. At the end of the debate you should be left with a sense of mutual respect. If not, the most important values are getting lost in arguments. Sex is overrated and way out of place when it comes to the higher values and attributes of sound relationships. Let us focus on those relational aspects that matter more and matter most.

SORROW

Make the most of your regrets; never smother your sorrow, but tend and cherish it till it comes to have a separate and integral interest. To regret deeply is to live afresh.

—Henry David Thoreau

SORROW

I can recall many times when I felt sorrow in my life. No one on this earth is without sorrow throughout life. There will always be events from time to time that are sorrowful. Loss of a friend or loved one, relationship difficulties, money problems, loss of a job, victim of a crime, or divorce, and this list can go on. One life strategy should be to make sure that you are not the cause of the situation that led to sorrow. Of course, if you are, sorrow offers an opportunity to assess the situation and take corrective action so that it does not happen again. Then again, there are situations that lead to sorrow which are out of our control. Is there any benefit to sorrow? Yes, there is. Times of sorrow prepare us to appreciate life and the people around us much more. In the hustle and bustle of life we oftentimes lose the ability to reflect and think more deeply about life, how we live and who we are. With this, sorrow opens up an opportunity to reflect on what matters most in life and take inventory of all the things and people to be grateful for. Sorrow can make you a more caring person towards others. Sorrow has no room for feelings of arrogance or other egotistical feelings. Sorrow therefore can make us humble and that is noticeable by others. Phases of sorrow can help us to see the good in others and bring out the good in us.

STIMULATION

The psychological basis of the metropolitan type of individuality consists in the intensification of nervous stimulation which results from the swift and uninterrupted change of outer and inner stimuli.

—Georg Simmel

STIMULATION

Have you ever watched an old black and white action movie and then compared it to modern day films and television? One thing you will notice with those old black and white films is that there is more lingering with a scene or dialogue and less switching views with the camera. Our span of attention has been shortened. This is compensated for by heightening the stimulation. It is an ever spiraling situation that has to be taken to the next level in order to keep the attention. We need to be aware of this impact on our span of attention. We are bombarded with all forms of stimulation. There is nothing wrong with stimulation unless it causes us to lose the ability to listen to each other attentively or concentrate on a topic, task or person. Over stimulation of any kind can create an imbalance. It can cause us to lose focus about what matters most. Over stimulation can lead to a superficial way of living.

TELEPHONES

I don't think the government is out to get me or help someone else get me but it wouldn't surprise me if they were out to sell me something or help someone else sell me something. I mean, why else would the Census Bureau want to know my telephone number?

—Andy Rooney

TELEPHONES

I find it rather fascinating when I see people with constant preoccupation with a phone. It seems we feel compelled to constantly check messages or make phone calls or check Facebook or whatever other website. It makes no difference where. It can be behind the wheel, waiting in line to pay for something, walking down the street. I can still recall the days when we had no cell phones and no computers. It felt like I had a greater awareness of things going on around me and had more opportunity to think when walking or driving. If I had down time, I had more time to read and have conversation with others that went beyond the brief sound bites on Facebook or text messaging. Be aware of this and make sure that it doesn't take over your life. Manage the times and frequencies of using your phone.

THINKING

Rarely do we find men who willingly engage in hard, solid thinking. There is an almost universal quest for easy answers and half-baked solutions. Nothing pains some people more than having to think.

—Martin Luther King, Jr.

THINKING

Who ever thought we would have to give some thought to thinking? If we did more thinking before acting or not taking action we probably would be experiencing less difficulties, problems and challenges. What does this tell you? Think! Think before you act and find the right questions to ask yourself before you act. Promote your thought processes by seeking sound advice and reading specialized literature. We live in an impulsive society. Ask the right questions and listen for the right answers. Is this right for me? Do I really need to buy this? Is this relationship healthy for me? Does this fit in with my long-term goals in life or is it going to interfere or keep me from achieving them? Once you recognize what is the right thing to do, act upon it courageously even though a part of you may resist because it is not the way you would usually respond. Learn to stop, reflect and think.

TIME

For disappearing acts, it's hard to beat what happens to the eight hours supposedly left after eight of sleep and eight of work.

—Doug Larson

TIME

I run into people constantly who say they don't have enough time. Time for what? Free time, time for family, vacation time, time for work, time to get that special project done, time to enjoy life. There is a time for everything. The key is to figure out how best to spend time. Time is one of our most valuable assets. Time, however, can only be spent. It cannot be saved for another day. What are we to do with this dilemma? The best thing to do is to spend time wisely. There are only twenty four hours in a day. No one has more, no one has less. Panic and stress will not add one single minute of time, in fact, it may detract from focusing and using your time properly.

TITILLATION

Beyond the beauty, the sex, the titillation, the surface, there is a human being. And that has to emerge.
—*Jeanne Moreau*

TITILLATION

Titillate is similar to: charge, electrify, excite, exhilarate, galvanize, intoxicate, pump up, thrill, turn on. These are the synonyms taken for the Merriam-Webster online dictionary. As with stimulate, titillate leads down a similar path although some may also associate pornography or strip clubs with this one. The same applies here. Whatever you fill your mind with in the way of titillation, there is less room for thoughts that are focused on those things that benefit society the most. Talk to our youth. They will tell you what's missing in us grownups. Our youth will tell you what they experienced at home that contributed to them getting into trouble or they end up in social circles of friends who are also taking the wrong road in life and experiencing similar trouble.

TRUTH

Anyone who doesn't take truth seriously in small matters cannot be trusted in large ones either.

—*Albert Einstein*

TRUTH

We have two choices. We can seek the truth or we can relativize the truth. What is your response when you are asked, "What is truth?" Do you respond with, "Truth is whatever you consider it to be." Some may say, "you've got your truth and I've got mine." How do they know that anyone has got truth? One thing for sure is that truth is the opposite of a lie or falsehood. I believe there are two types of truth, absolute truth and perceived truth. Absolute truth is sovereign and independent of what you and I may consider to be true even though, from time to time, perceived truth may be the same. Absolute truth is what we should constantly seek and strive for to make sure that our perceived truth does not become a roadblock and we remain open to possibly being wrong about what we consider to be true. To find truth you must be very honest about who you are and accept the basic premise of following the highest natural law of treating others as you would like to be treated. If the basic premise of the Golden Rule is not applied, you will probably find a different truth wherever you look.

TELEVISION

I find television to be very educating. Every time somebody turns on the set, I go in the other room and read a book.

—Groucho Marx

TELEVISION

It is interesting to take a look at what was said about television when it first hit the market back in the 1940s. In 1947 there were 44,000 television sets in American homes, most in New York City. TV was a mysterious way to bring others into your home where you listen and see them. It was a one way conversation though. The TV talked. All you could do was listen. Let me ask you this question. If all that you learned about life, jobs, relationships, finances and other areas of your life was only through TV, would you be all the wiser? Would you be more informed? Would you be learning solid values that benefit you and others? Or would you predominantly be learning how to live an egotistical life where everything is about you. What are the values portrayed on television? Are you learning how to respectfully debate issues of importance or are you learning how to be confrontational and treat anyone who does not agree with you as the "enemy" or not worthy of associating with or even speaking to? My advice to you is to limit and minimize your television time. Firstly, it could kill you because you may not be getting enough exercise. Secondly, too much television will poison the mind with superficiality and life values that are not healthy and could lead to brain atrophy.

WORK

Whatever your life's work is, do it well. A man should do his job so well that the living, the dead, and the unborn could do it no better.
—Martin Luther King, Jr.

WORK

When I was ten or eleven years old there lived a disabled military veteran down the street who was a writer but not able to use his hands so he recorded his manuscripts and they would then be typed by someone else. He had a disease called MS or multiple sclerosis. He needed someone to read his manuscripts for an hour or two a couple of days a week. Since we were already acquainted, I was interviewed by the Veterans Administration and was accepted for the job. This gave me an early sense of work ethic and responsibility and the veteran Army major had a great sense of humor despite his disability.

Work imparts dignity and therefore makes one feel good about him- or herself. Work is also a social environment where we learn to interact with others and collaborate as a team to accomplish the tasks at hand. Work of course has the purpose of providing what is needed for food and a place to stay.

There may be times when we become unemployed which can have a devastating psychological impact. However, this is also an opportunity to do some soul searching and giving thanks for what we do have. Facing the work place with an attitude of wanting to help your employer and co-workers is the kind of employee that employers are looking for. While job searching, be willing to do any kind of job in the interim to keep some cash flowing.

About the Author

Bob Weinstein
Lt. Colonel, US Army, Retired
www.BeachBootCamp.net

BIO

Born in Washington, D.C., **Joseph "Bob" Weinstein** grew up in Virginia and spent 20 years in Berlin, Germany; he is retired from the United States Army as a Lieutenant Colonel with 30 years of service and spent about half that time as a senior military instructor with the Command & General Staff College.

He has been featured on radio and television, among others, on the History Channel and Fox Sports Net as well as in various publications such as the Washington Times, The Miami Herald and the Las Vegas Tribune.

His background is unique and diverse, including: military instructor, attorney, motivational speaker, wellness coach, certified corporate trainer, and certified personal trainer. He is fluent in German and English.

He is a popular motivational speaker at corporate events and banquets and conducts military-style workouts on Fort Lauderdale Beach utilizing strength, cardio, flexibility and agility training - both in personal training and group sessions.

He strongly believes in the importance of giving back to the community. Colonel Weinstein has volunteered his time for homeless and run-away kids at the Covenant House and also devotes time to training youth who are members of the US Naval Sea Cadets Corps, Team Spruance, Fort Lauderdale, Florida.

He is a member of the American Council on Exercise, Military Officers Association and Veterans of Foreign Wars..

He is the author of *Boot Camp Fitness for All Shapes and Sizes* as well as many other books. Some of his previous clients as a guest speaker include: Sony, DHL, American Express, KPMG, AOL, IBM, AARP, SmithBarney, Green Bay Packers and Humana.

Joseph "Bob" Weinstein
Lt. Colonel, US Army, Retired
954-636-5351
www.BeachBootCamp.net

Books and Other Products by
Bob Weinstein
Lt. Colonel, US Army, Retired
www.BeachBootCamp.net

Boot Camp Fitness for All Shapes and Sizes
Paperback, $19.95, 265 pages, ISBN 978-0-9841783-1-5
EBook, $9.95, ISBN 978-0-984-17837-7 (all formats)

Weight Loss - Twenty Pounds in Ten Weeks
Paperback, $18.95, 220 pages, ISBN 978-0-9841783-0-8
EBook, $9.99, ISBN 978-0-984-17834-6 (all formats)

Quotes to Live By
Paperback, $11.95, ISBN 978-0-9841783-2-2
EBook, $5.95, ISBN 978-0-984-17833-9 (all formats)

Discover Your Inner Strength (co-author)
Paperback, $19.95
Ebook, $9.95, ISBN 978-0-984-17836-0

Food & Fitness Journal
Paperback, $14.95, 212 pages, ISBN 978-1-935759-03-4
Ebook, $4.95, ISBN 978-1-935759-06-5

Six Keys to Permanent Weight Loss
Audio book as MP3 download (Amazon), 60 minutes
$6.93

Eight Secrets to Longevity, Health and Fitness
Audio book as MP3 download (Amazon), 50 minutes
$8.91

Health Colonel Boot Camp T-Shirts, Mugs, etc.
Go to www.cafepress.com/healthcolonel to order online
Other books by Health Colonel Publishing:
The Tale of the Little Duckling by Grit Weinstein
Paperback, $14.95, picture book story for 4 to 8 year olds
ISBN 978-0-9841783-8-4
EBook, $5.99, ISBN 978-0-984-17839-1 (all formats)

Quotes, Wisdoms and Some Dumb Things

www.ingramcontent.com/pod-product-compliance
Lightning Source LLC
Chambersburg PA
CBHW032359040426
42451CB00006B/63